signature 476/500

Black Pepper Special Editions

Black Pepper First Edition handsigned
and numbered by the author

476/500

DEAR B

DEAR B

Jennifer Harrison

Black Pepper

© Jennifer Harrison 1999

First published by *Black Pepper*
403 St Georges Road, North Fitzroy, Victoria 3068

All rights reserved

National Library of Australia

Cataloguing-in-Publication data:

Harrison, Jennifer, 1955-
    Dear B.

    ISBN 1 876044 27 6

    1. Title

A821.3

Cover design: Gail Hannah

This project has been assisted by the Commonwealth Government, through the Australia Council, its art funding and advisory body.

Printed and bound by Arena Printing and Publishing
35 Argyle Street, Fitzroy, Victoria 3065

Acknowledgements

Poems in this book have been published in *Meanjin*, *Going Down Swinging*, *Voices*, and *Divan*. The sequence entitled Diary was selected for inclusion in the Anti-Cancer Council's Literary Exhibition at the National Gallery of Victoria, 1997.

Grateful acknowledgement is also made to the Literature Board of the Australia Council for financial support.

Contents

The Getting of Wisdom	1
Sewing	2
Lightning Ridge	3
Agate	4
Husk	6
The Light Itself	7
Superstition	8
Hippocrates	9
Boston Poems	10
Arriving	10
Diary	11
Boston Gallery	16
New Year's Eve, Boston Common	17
White Boston	17
Newbury Street	18
That Place	19
The Thought	20
Picture	22
Diarist	23
The Abbey	24
Embryo	25
Doubtful Sound	26
Dear B	28
Freud's Daughter Writes a Story Called Revenge	35
Baron von Munchausen	36
The Society of Psychotherapist's Fantasy Ball	37
Stanton Welch's *Cinderella*	38
The Remains of the Day	39
Miniatures	40
Out of Body Experience	45
Wall	46

Mountains of the Moon	47
Lot's Wife	48
Local Astronomy	52
The Emperor Tamarin	53
In The Park	55
A Serious Case	56
Botanical Gardens	57
Bridesmaid 19 Times and Never a Bride	58
The Bridge	60
Ceremony	62
The Question Mark	63
Casino	64

For Bruce

The Getting of Wisdom

As my mother said,
If you don't ask you won't learn
the squeaky wheel gets oiled
and then again don't trust men
who wear white dress-up shoes.
Always carry money for a phone-call
and never go to bed without reconciliation
that was one of my grandmother's
favourites. Treat others as you'd have
done unto you, never boil abalone
in the presssure cooker, a little Ajax
on the teeth for whiteness, we'll buy
them a present but let's only give it
to them if they've got one for us.

Sewing

Am I late he asked
arriving late, behind him
the small deaths of each town
he had passed, in his eyes
the tired light as it had, all day,
fallen across the tar's curve
as it had burned at sunset
across the farmlands and fences
the dry paddocks and
the rivers' nodal esturaries
until evening, when,
in anticipation
of lessening distances,
of tomorrows beginning freshly,
he had hurried home,
late, to she
who, by the fire sewing,
had turned to him
who asked.

Lightning Ridge

Shale heaps picked clean of opal chips.
Children pan for potch in an ocean of rubble.
Sprinklers create an oval of green
for the dogs. And the sun drinks colour from fences.

An emblem of the town's history,
a shack made of beer bottles becomes a museum.
Easy to imagine someone down on their luck
slapping the cement on an empty.

And the wildest parties? You see them
in those parts of the wall which tilt like crazy talking
about the black opal flecked with blood that lies
in the earth, in the dregs, in the wattle.

Agate
— in 1709, a Brazilian priest invented an airship containing an agate which he believed would fly to heaven

Today she reads about tiny agates
inscribed with verses,
the Koran written into toe-rings
herdsmen crossing the desert.

Priests invent their airships
obsessing over faith
but she thinks of the usual advice
given in regard to old mines:
>   KEEP OUT.

Her metaphors share the career
of other river gravels; they are carried along
and, according to the Romans, we were all
to be skilled in carving cameos.

Penderecki flies further
than the sun's thunder egg
further than mineral lovers
imprisoned in green chrysophase.

A fossicker
spikes his violent gad into the land
— now he loves the gem
gently with tweezers
>   as though it were a heart
suddenly lonely in the human palm.

Invincible, held
within ropes of chalcedony,
a blue agate from Agate Creek
— the eye of a Queensland cyclops.

Lucky strikes apart, theft is usually
a straight forward political pick up.
Delight, here, is to read the past first
and then the future.

She writes: a moss agate made of grey
milky silica whose ferny designs
resemble the hennaed skin
of the poetess Mirabai.

Husk

Your nervous heart insists
that lightness makes sense of grace
that boneless time weighs the seed and
spills its morse as choreography
now prisoner stammering
in the breathless crevice — fly fly
across flagstones: smooth
tumbling brief - pinned now
to the ragged branch
you disappear longing to see.

The Light Itself

Everywhere it touched
the light left a transparent woman.
Even to speak of it
spills more tremor and
gritty as eggshells,
motes form
beneath closed lids.
All day safe words
have run from the tremble
from nerve ends
more brittle than colour.
Reading Akhmatova
the *White Flock Poems*
and *Reed*, furious embryos
push worlds from hiding
...see cluster
and husk and tiny cup...no
that's not right...we are used
to this riot, swelling
in the bright street light
the looting of style and type.

Superstition

Clothes collect the body's form
from failures
buttons find their holes

I can't recall if the creature spoke
nor if its many mouths of clay
found mine

The ghoul they call the self-segmenter
memorised
all the moods of the moon

And whispered in my ear
"Enter here
for I am the green sea"

I woke
but flames had kept nothing at bay
and on my arm a tattoo glistened

A blue woman
a serpent
crushed beneath her tiny inked feet.

Hippocrates

He has looked into the well
and seen the unwell drowning.
Carotids bleed between his thumbs.
He listens stooped like a bean
for the heart's rumble.
His caress rescues and discards
...those pale methodical eyes
which have been indoors so long...

Sometimes he is afraid
of everything that ends
— the corpse falling always
into mossy flight, towards
the cool drinkable water
which resists fate
and gives death only its power

Primum non nocere
first do no harm...poets, too

Boston Poems

Arriving

It was always arriving, although we didn't realise
until it had arrived, how far
it had travelled, how weary the cancer must have been
to sleep so tenderly, not bothering anyone

and how quickly the word
fitted our lives, easily, as the Charles river
or Thanksgiving or the story of Martin Luther King

how it crept along the soul
like a shadow on Newbury St

and drank Paul Revere's painted vine of blood
so that the Freedom Trail
would be remembered by the children who followed
 after.

It must have been arriving, always,
for your hand to know most surely
when and where it would declare its thirst

(a traveller like us making excursions
into cultures we trust will
accommodate our oddities)

now I read my children the happiest stories
and not the ones I didn't believe at the time
about the disappointed woman

who, when she thought ahead,
swore that her numbers cried blood.

I disembark at Copley
and push through the turnstile
behind a boy with a map and backpack
who turns to me for directions.

I confuse his arriving eyes with mine
and point him towards the Pei building
where the city reflects liquidly
in the largest mirror known.

> *Diary*
> *Boston, October 1990 - June 1991*

*

I take the news on a black telephone

I write down a list of things I will do
to make my life clean

you hold me like a circle
like a clock

I sew the hem of a dress
and now you keep away

knowing
that sometimes a kindness can break me

*

tremulous hands
wheelchairs in Outpatients

a coffee-machine
plastic thimbles
filled with milk

a sense that until now
I've been ignorant
of how blue the sky can be
glimpsed through a high window

a sense of horses
quietly grazing

I talk with nurses
about the weather

and a young girl
leaves chocolates on the table
for the doctors to eat

*

become quiet now

listen to this man's hand
on my breast

I want him to auscultate my heart
with careful ears

divide good
from bad with his scalpel

I trust he knows my name
that he knows my left
from my right

that he knows for this journey
I will need to sleep deeply
without dreams

but I don't trust him
how can I trust any longer
anything I feel or say?

I ask questions
but more arrive
later when I'm at home
alone in the dark with my cells

   *

memories
lie down in a sweet place

lie down
memories

memories: my pregnant womb
calm as the sea at dawn

lie down good memories
drift me to sleep

*

the anaesthetist's temple
throbs like a drug

he has a woodsman's jaw
and the strong arms of a masked man

a dark forest whispers
in the promised needle

I lie down in the trees
he is above me
as though for the first time

I am awake
I am awake
   mother

*

stop the car
I must walk for a while
by the lake

you winter
you moth-eaten rug of ice

you husband, strange man
Stop the Car

I must scream
but I don't want you
to hear

only the ice

stop the car
I want this howl
to shatter every blade of glass

*

you say that you don't want
to outlast me
but of course

you must want to
you are my lover
of lies
thank you

the black angel
knows both our names
but lies will keep us safe

*

chrome and beige, black metal
one ton, two million dollars worth
of precision instrument

daily 10.45 to 11.15 am
straker, licker of nipple tips

you sliding up and over
shooting Chernobyl
from a silent shrivel gun

lie just nice, tattoos measured
in place, don't move
good, be good, be a good girl

you wrap-around smile
everything I hate
control-freak machine
you radiotherapy

don't forget
everyday I walk out on you
everyday I walk out on you
and don't look back, tomorrow

Boston Gallery

Even the cars seem to shiver.
On the lake the swan boats have frozen
but you tell yourself it will seem like summer
once you get there. You have visions of colour
images nailed by names to all the walls.

Inside the gallery, a room is filled
with World War II bomber planes
each ply-wood plane the size of a finger.
In the second room, abstract fish
montage the tropics from floor to ceiling.

Outside sheer glass windows
rain hammers its sleety installation.
Across the snow blurred shapes of cars and trees
the wind kicks and kicks
as we swim aimlessly through guarded rooms
like similar fish in similar boots
through air.

New Year's Eve, Boston Common

Air burns breath to smoke
and the wind stabs lancelot spears
through our cellophane coats.
Here, New Year
is ice sculptures in the park
fireworks exploding
across grey-eyed sky.
Children scratch their names into puddles.
Strangers hug each others gloves.
Shots of bourbon burn like Sydney.
I stay past midnight
when the kissing starts.

White Boston

Evening slides through mist
leans across the city's stone bridges.
Buttonwood trees, the dry scent of snow.

Bell-chimes, crisp as linen and
a church spire white as a whale's spout
"slumbering on the Norway foam."

White star, white spot of the basilisk —
the true description of white
contains all the shades of dissent.

My friend asks where are the blacks in Boston?
She's looking around for a place to live
after Chicago.

Then we walked to the river
where, under floodlights, the evening skaters
scratch circles
into the beautiful hardness of ice.

Newbury Street

It was an expedition
to walk from one shop to the next
but the climber needs another visit to see
everything from adolescence to death.

Love can't be a street
beginning with inventiveness
heading for a view of the lake
— Ritz or Hilton on the park?

History pins names to cafes and fountains.
Magnolias open white throats.
Oil in the occasional eye flickers
a rebellion, I suppose, against anonymity.

Behind iron-handled doors, women
have kicked off their shoes and
lie idling through the rooms of their lives.
Anything less than a riot would not be love.

Which facade presumes something other
to be true? Only the flower vendors call
to reassure, their scented gardens
offering lips, wrapped and dew-laden.

That Place

Do you remember that place in Revere
which sells the live lobsters
and soft panda bears

where we stopped on a whim
suddenly hungry for the absurd American juke box
crouched like a buddha in every booth?

the songs followed one another
so that nobody drank beer alone
nobody talked without an echo

and the lyrics leaned in close
mortality puzzling us only a little
and we went on finding a joke to share

we pressed those well-thumbed buttons
and all the time you were looking
at the colourful plastic strips in the doorway

while I was watching the ceiling fan
turn slowly as though in a fake breeze
like a seagull might, over jetty guts.

The Thought

Not that I expect you to wait
for this illness to pass
because unlike dreams
we are turning left or right
or staying still.
We are walking over
our smoking battlefields
burning our feet on the dry ice
of new and positive doctrines.
Evolving from the fabulous world
of feathers we fall into ourselves
slowly accompanying
regret through the air.

If there is a riddle to decipher
it will not despair of its own
enigma. The thought of a cat
can be more silky than the fur itself.
The thought of love can rise
each day to reacquaint itself with
the neighbours of a house
which would explain
why somedays we unravel
and others we sit
close to each other
our eyebrows very still
above the milky books.

Picture

The old woman can't fix anything enough.
She wheels her barrow back and forth after dark
stopping to check the pulse
of three girls who stand in a doorway talking.

She takes her brush. Adds handbags.
Breasts wearing their shoulder straps long.
She whites out the wooden boats, the sails
ploughing through waves, noise

of heaving, foaming, lone gull crying.
She dabs the sky with turpentine
and softens the stars which dive once
into her mouth and are hardened forever.

Diarist

Her great age signifies a secret province
a lack of restraint. There is no map.
Soon time will cease to signal
and urgency will dash itself from a cliff.
Some pattern of her body, previously numb
a hormone or a system, will overpower
her hold on memory. Her fingers will not slip.
She'll be describing a third party, a white noise.
She won't follow a memory to its source
nor a thought to its conclusion. She'll be
constructing a topography, an incidental grid
a landscape say that is ultimately sensual
as she beckons us into a red and glowing tunnel
handing us poems like coals to throw on brittle grasses.

The Abbey

In the cloistered ruin, novices
share their thoughts with silence
their bare feet whisper upon stone.
Birds feed from the window-sills.

All day the sun considers the solitary path
(chosen on a whim, fashioned, at least
in the beginning, by worldly concerns)
of the few who begin to know themselves
by the absence of a city.

Their skirts tear on briars
noticed only for the blackness of the fruit.
If I were to say the river has broken its bank
they would open their laps
and cradle my lips which speak the truth.

Embryo

A maintenance free area
blends into bushscape, native
seedling, nature poem
imitating the velvet rust plant.
I will have to prune
these notes and make a hole
in the bush for broken stone
to see how a lawn is made
but carefully: the loss of one root
may mean
the dropping of many branches.
Whether or not we belong
at the edges of wilderness
are we ready to differentiate
ourselves from nature
not knowing what will be
delivered
once the heart's primordial tube
begins to doubt?

Doubtful Sound

I

Tarnished grey as an heirloom, the lake
breathes quietly in morning light.
A low brown town huddles on the cusp
energised by a Gothic tracery of birds.

Drifting wood at the water's edge
your arms make a chunky branch
your parka hood, a bowl
for the Manapouri rain which falls whispering.

I hear you calling to come and see
the fossil you have found in the sand
but I have entered the waterfall, far
across the lake where, deafened by snow

in free-falling, giddy descent, stung by air
the valley comes rushing to meet me
with shocking hands
and a lap full of *tangiwai* stone.

II

Rockpools dispel our reflections.
In the blue lake of Te Anau
in the glow worm caves of Eglington
shadows labelled with our own names

pass us by like foreign places.
Something frets and cannot hold
the cave's light in the moment's rain
despite good news of love.

Sheer granite batholiths
tower above *toetoe*, lichen
above ferns swaying on stems
of black glass.

Dead trees draped with mistletoe
line the road and shake
their feather boas as though to sigh
why do you come? what is there to see?

And still the waterfalls plunge
into the Tasman and always the rain
these nights we wake like animals disturbed
by the same dream of downpour.

Dear B

Dear B

I'm writing a path through the mountains
through the Himalayan snows
and the 8 trekking days of April 1980
we are walking from Pokara to Jomson
down river one day
up valley the next
in small huts at night
we lie among the sleeping chickens
beside children wrapped
in the warm body of their mother

Dear B

I'm writing a path through the mountains
to the Nepali house
where the goat's carcass hangs
in the doorway
brushing our shoulders each time we pass
where the beds are straw
and the shadows flicker
and dung fires
reach for the cold moon
rising over river pebbles

I'm writing a path through the mountains
to the festival of Holi
the stone walls of the village
are splashed with dye

so that the the village
which bleeds bleeds all day
to the sound of laughter
and the smell of clay-baked bread
when children throw a bucket of dye
over you
you are stained with the first blood
of a woman
and I taste you like a ceremony
I don't understand what it is
to be foreign

Dear B

I'm not afraid of the cold
of walking the stones
like the saddhu we meet
who carries fossils from Muktinath
his ammonites are basalt listening
foetuses
and the donkeys are sure-footed as birds
their bells ringing
their dress feathers flaring
like rhododendrens
against the Annapurnas

I walk beside an old woman
whose wrists and neck are thin
as wire
she carries five foot planks of timber
across her shoulders, eggs
in her forehead basket
to the village of Tatapani
four days ahead

one foot before the other
like a metronome
a woman of strength
and broken rice sweetness
her tendons
hard as the ropes across her forehead
have worn these stones
to their smoothness

Dear B

rest now
the old woman has passed by
I lie in the hot springs
of Tatapani
aching muscles caressed
by the earth's core
I slip into a scalding day dream
algael medicines
steam each pore open
and when I plunge into the icy river
the shocking cold
burns a cave into my skin
inside this pain
is the single flame ·
which loves you

Dear B

for ten days now
we have been stranded in Jomson
with the Swiss and Germans
we are waiting for the plane

which can't land we
are helpless out of place here
where the wind has tasted Niligiri's ice
we are shivering, afraid
of the snow leopards, the snow crows
we are so close to heaven
yet argue
over who will wear the blanket
we once shared on warmer nights
further down the valley

we eat and sleep and shiver
and there is a dead body on a stretcher
waiting for better weather
to journey down to the grave
down to Tolkein's terraced plains
where he wrote *The Hobbit*
here we might die
among the evil fairies we conjure
because we are so far from home

Dear B

can you see the apple trees
planted by American Aid Abroad?
they are saplings staked in tidy rows
Junga tells us that one day
the villagers will make apple sauce
and brandy
to sell to the tourists

the apple trees
are battered by the blizzard
sleet chills the bones
of the American apple trees
the wind's invisible fists
flinging the idea of an apple
into the river below
where torrents cut through rock
like the blood of Kali
destroyer of dreams

when the apple trees die
they will plant new ones
so that I think of Eve
and the beginning of gardens
the storm screaming
for the rib he wants back

Dear B

do you remember the German
whose feet had festered
with frostbite
in whose eyes we saw the grey ache
of death
despite all his technical gear
and stranded money?

when you found
4 vials of ancient penicillin
in a disused apothecary shack
at the edge of the village

you carried them gently
through the snow
so that they did not shatter
and the German wept

later he sent you a photo
of his feet
only one toe missing
this is how he loved you
convalescing
a little of himself
lost
taken by Nepal

Dear B

I'm writing a path through memory
and it's as though I send you
a photograph of ourselves years ago
Machupuchare in the background
in the foreground: Junga
wearing the striped sweater
I should have let him keep
and your tall shadow slipping
at sunset
between tussocks of grass
outside, now, when the wind blows
it is September in Melbourne
and we wake each dawn in a brick house
the spring rains have arrived
after two dry winters

when I dreamt last night
I dreamt of an old woman carrying
wood to Tibet
she was carving a path through the mountains
she was descending
ascending
she was going away

tonight I can't sleep
as though a fever
has transpired from the dream

I think I must write this down
now before morning
before I forget

Freud's Daughter Writes a Story Called Revenge

Her words, sparse hurricanes
push the sky way beyond
the horizons I meant for her.
Beyond what I might think she knows
she's entered the head of a murderer
and I see how she's watched the news for clues
how well her story is written — an A
for a massacre. She travels so easily
no excess prophecy — youthfulness is like that —
the grace of torpedoes pushing through sugar —
the consequences somewhere else.
She's disobeyed grief and captured
the horror in a web of sad spiders.
Alert to her attentive alchemy
I might any moment write, myself, something new
but the bullet's breath grazes eternity
and the death instinct has always frightened me.

Baron von Münchhausen

Please don't confuse me with that rogue Raspe.
I'm not a "type" of tall story nor
would I steal the Landgraf gems
after discovering *Ossian* and publishing Percy.
I'm a more modest braggart something like
the marvellous lover who cannot say goodbye
or the cavalry captain always throwing a party
on the perpetual eve of leaving for Russia.
And who would insist I put down my helmet and lance
to sleep the same soft sleep as the committed man?
The truth is I exaggerate what I know
and the story I tell is the truth in disguise.
If a suspicious tree takes root in your forehead
remember that I'm rich and noble. I'm the Baron of Lies.

The Society of Psychotherapist's Fantasy Ball

Freud wore a long skirt slit to his thigh
    so the stocking top could be seen when he sat.
The wallflower was, by comparison, quixotic.

She surfaced in the fiction of Kristeva
    and was pale, unrequited - she grew
as tangled ivy into the cracks of Anna's wall.

Melanie dreamed of Sherlock Holmes scavenging
    through a graveyard of dolls, her
good and bad breasts clues to his deductive position.

Lacan hid a conceptual trail of cracked china cups
    embroidered shawls, knitted sandals; he
mocked Kernberg who played dice and cards all evening.

Gypsies hoodwink you, cheat you daily
    said the behaviourists who ate all the smoked salmon
at supper leaving Winnicott the biryani

which was good enough. But I was telling you about
    the wallflower who was in love with a sleuth...
in the process, in the real fiction

dancing in ever-widening folk dresses
    the self-help book snaps open and shut, the chinks
in theory now so overgrown with narrative

you'd never know where to find a neurosis' thirsty roots.

Stanton Welch's *Cinderella*

He's given the ghosts the same
spotlight as the living.
He's given them
point shoes, a romantic dance
of their own in the Second Act.
He's given the dead
clever choreography
a coffin for Rimbaud's heart
a worm for the slipper's lost foot.
He's given the dancers a look
at the body the dancer will become.
He's given the forest its litter
gender its genderlessness.
And the ghosts, the ghosts!
See them swaying
like a grass of spines?
Surprise completes the fable.
She marries the Pauper not the Prince.
There's no point compromising
and here she goes
holding hands with chance again
barefoot, brave, a woman, the same.

The Remains of the Day

A butler priest
walks beneath rosary stars
stifling the scuffle of his heart

When the trapped bird fell
his rooms were thick with drapery
and destined to panic

Did he see himself groaning down
through layers of propriety
to her the first mirror
in which he saw a future
withheld?

His English mansions
glide into the air
returning always to the same hand
that sends them
skywards

To the hand of the master
who laughed
when the trapped bird fell.

Miniatures

notes while reading The Tale of Genji *by Murasaki Shikibu*

*

a cellophane salmon curls in my palm
I am a jealous type, not superstitious

*

infidelity is a code, a chromosome
.0512 cell river/flood plain

*

the mathematical heart
is not infinite

*

but of the pulse again, the self-help clinic
and artificial sleep...please come soon

*

islands drift away
but I have fingers, an exoskeleton

*

quivering in pale sand
a soldier crab burrows sideways

*

and every night, so I'm told
I repeat in my sleep a word...

*

not time, not love, not place
their insoluble "have" and "had"

*

the market-crowd, the milling blade
minutes spin to the wall like grass

*

as if you never did touch the floor
of the Luna Park Rotor...where's my shoe?

*

as if you were left after dark, still spinning
stuck to the wall, here is the news:

*

a top finds its centre more or less
automatically

*

birds fly past
in circles; I am not nauseous

*

nausea —
the wad of unpaid bills, surly as a ditch

*

we end the sweaty day...
and odd to think, asleep

*

he slid down the wall, his silk shirt
a blossoming parachute above his shoulders

*

networks chip away, communicate at grief
The Age: a clever chilly poem

*

if you remember, time forgot
retrieves you now, intact, colluding

*

lilac racemes, wisteria leaves
bees, black honey...the argument carries on

*

language: a batik scarf of trees
throws out shadows into the Pacific

*

throws out and about
wind punch &/or a colonial nature?

*

surgeons clamp arteries, their tongs
sweetening the body

*

in houses stacked along streets
in streets stacked around mountains, beaches flinch

*

the rest is blown away
my oscilloscope collapses like a toy

*

bandaged iridiums, strips
of light return to a bird's wing

*

more than ever, briefly, in between
I am a spectrum...thank you, again, I don't smoke

*

the winter is harsh
but I heat quickly in the cracked pot

*

among the translocations
and sea-lilies — where are you?

*

damn it — we arranged to meet
on Sunday...at 2 o'clock...the pet shop is closed

*

where's my leather jacket? my sun glasses? don't
...it's safe...I'm not mad at you

*

something shuts down quite suddenly
like the flash of computer parts shorting out?

*

a trauma; silence
could be, after all, a severe improvement

*

especially social? no, suppose
that, indoors, Murasaki is talking

*

of food, poetry, the strange behaviour
of waiting — ah here you are! on time

Out of Body Experience

Last night I lay above myself in the dark
looking down upon a stranger beside him.
Momentarily, in the moonlight, she was that person
I am no more, the one seen from far away
who cannot be regained or changed
and whom the dawn will not unite.
The two women who lie awake beside him
cannot speak or touch each other.
One is made of earth and blood, the other
of air and moon-frost. All the night between them
is past and future night
so that everything I have done, everything she watches
becomes a memory, now passing
as I sleep and wake outside her, inside myself, beside him.

Wall

One green or another
both sides of a story
iron their creases
and rise gleaming
either side of the wall.
Does it matter
birds skim the unmade bed
of the sea's slim vigilance?
Now a boy stands to ride
the wave of the blouse
unbuttoned, the ocean
ribs bare to the dare of
land. One blue or another
we are unbuckled colour
licking the clouds alive.

Mountains of the Moon
the movie documents the life of explorer Richard Burton
the italicised lines are from Rumi

You will never find a more Nilish Nile
than the clues I leave for you
so subtly in camp-fire smoke
in the African flesh you press so tenderly
to your gentleman's breast.
Did you think you would leave me
desolate, awash with love *this day*
you and we are fallen into a whirlpool
who knows how to swim?
I'm a woman who wears her jaguar tooth
sealed in silver, I tumble over rocks.
I live underground. Mountains of the Moon.

Lot's Wife

I

She looks for Zoar but sees nothing left.
She looks nowhere. Her god is dead.
She can't find the road of daughters.
She can't find her name or the details of her birth.
In her anonymous wilderness
of Dead Sea pillars, she
can't touch the cooking pot
or sort the bundled hemp.
She unwraps and sorts the look of death
the look ahead, the look of breath
but can't undo her hair or scarf
or claim her way or find the sun
or check her pockets for the forgotten key.
She looks for Zoar, the gate, the end
the emotion he had packed, unpacked
for her, back then.

More petrified than ever before
she paces inside her sea-shell calm.
What can she do to undo fear?
She can only look.

II

Sad sadness. A woman in love
with the sea has no secrets.
Even her name holds nothing lucidly
sand over sand
waves looking back
fierce in their salt sling.
Such negligence, to be a statue.
Such an easy sleep to watch
the graceful centuries
bring news of foam
and suck shells out
while weeds drag sky
down into oblivion.
She has all the ancient instincts:
hunger, vertigo, grief
but see how her abstracts creep
back across the reef?
She's tricked us all with
solid rot defying form, no urge
but that which bows to hers.
Such greediness to be a statue.
Winter eagles dive
for the good town left behind
but she's on her own watching
the tide come in.

No more stuttering under moons
in the margins of tepid dunes Lot.
Waves bleed such pale foam.
Tomorrow, find my clothes
by the Dead Sea
my footsteps leading to the nearest village.

   III

I've been ambiguous
I've lied about my motives
I've smoked a cigarette
I've burned my palms
with the well bucket
I've sorted olives
and scented men
You might say I'm not so different
from other women
I've looked into puddles
and seen my face shatter
and reform
I've looked into the fire
of purple desires
curling around blistered wood
you might say I'm exactly
the shape of anticipation
verses
will not describe the forces
which did not destroy me

In the margins
of a slightly-known text
I am a paradox
I look behind I look ahead
curious to see
what I am to be next.

Local Astronomy

Even so, the spellcheck can't pick out
those mistakes we've meant to fix
for an age now. The fig trees of Europe
are ragged, bald with virus.
We have our own die-back though
and the local astronomy above our heads
to believe in - Darwin
versus the spirit of the universe -
the little splutter a machine makes
when we try to be clever.
Ships inch along the horizon
beneath sniff-lines of smoke
and the driftwood weathered smooth, up close
is the thigh-bone of an animal
washed down by flood to the estuary.
And I can't help this girl
who keeps on walking into my pictures
with her lilac blouse
and nervous captaincy
pushing instincts into line.
She'll stop somewhere in the middle of a storm
in the middle of a scrawl, a cheerful thought
in the middle of a cheeful line,
perfectly spelled, hopefully.

The Emperor Tamarin

When you read this morning that last night
    the emperor tamarin was stolen from the Melbourne zoo
you thought it was yesterday again that

a tragedy was happening in the elsewhere news
    but then tomorrow you read about it
in the news you must believe

and find that you are part of conversations
    you didn't mean to hear - at work
or on the train to work or in the tram.

Every *perhaps did you know I heard it first
    this morning before*, gives you the feeling
that everything has happened already a little bit ago

and that living in the world
    is like browsing through advertisements or
watching a river slide by through a glass bottom boat.

It is and isn't the headlines you dread —
    denial can't rescue a child unscathed
from an unfenced pool or murderous paedophile —

and mostly you crave the happiest news
    — such as alert security finding the tamarin
last night in the recycle bins of Mentone MacDonald's

When you thought it was yesterday again that
    a tragedy was happening in the somewhere news
you were at home at the time

somewhere else you were lost in thought
    with no place to go, you were moving through
the clamour, unused to freedom, unsure of the corner.

In the Park

Her daughter loves to swing in the park
"Swing me. Swing me higher than you"
and her mother swings her across the mown grass
the swing slap-slapping her hands

in the park, Larkin's women
are not pushed to the side of their lives
they cup shoulders and hips
in hard enamelled palms
their thick arms working in the rhythm of the sea

and the blood once fed to their wombed young.
Washed, washed, they are the symmetry
of holding, the realm of the swing
colours washing through the sun.

A Serious Case

The sunset eclipses recitation
and thinking about thinking
is the umbilical inheritance
which palls as it means

pinpointing the question
sand sticks to your skin
and the shoreline's fragments
wash their confessions

over and over
in the pianola manner
the plan itself
will be superceded

by something returning
to Marx or a more cynical concept
mashed from the epigrams
of dailiness

we change form dismiss the obsolete
at least under the microscope
entropies bloom as flowers
and terraines silvery as ice

push their nuclear pebbles
sourcewards
love being, as always
both genetic and religious.

Botanical Gardens

In the trees they're rigging lights
for *A Midsummer Night's Dream*

and tonight Poe's bats will fly
across the moon towards St Kilda pier

through gate C&D, the city's lung
sucks in and out the waspish air

as children strive to see
the dramatists' names

scrawled on coppery plaques
hidden in the bushes

ducks surround an old woman breaking bread
grass prickles my cheek like a fine steel carpet

in the pond a lily floats without a stem
how elegant it would be —

if not for the man in joggers, loitering
he, too, has been planted here among the species.

Bridesmaid 19 Times and Never a Bride

tiny fish swerve
through pools reminding her
of a corps de ballet seen years ago
in Surfer's Paradise

the thought of waves made visible
to the outstretched ear: *I do*
the sound itself
a sequinned woman gliding
down aisles of faith

bridesmaid 19 times
and never a bride, she
has married her soul's best man
he who watches from the periphery

of ceremony, of acquiesence
she knows nothing
her ecstasies have upped and walked away
maligned by a truthful verb
the infinite *to be*

her eyes lucky opals, sifted out
will they sell plucked out
in a bowl among the rituals?

she's serious - this bride to be
of happiness
who has stopped midway at a garden
who will turn back now

without inheriting
his cavalry
the blunt toes of his camels and rivers

the bride to be of swans
her visceral self shoaled
on a shelf of pearl

she cannot be more precise
than a grain of rice thrown
as poor man's money
a ritual
carved from the bone of her family

what use has she for guests appearing
as pencils of colour
for token garters
and blue borrowings?

she is serious this bride to be
of idiosyncracy, this cradler of veils
and holder of shadows

on the lounge, in the easy chair
she is too dangerous to say *I do.*

The Bridge
in memoriam, Andrew Ziolkowsky

Easily symmetry is wrenched apart
and now it's plain that we will never
wholly be on this or that side of a bridge
or a government.
The wind lashing Milson's point
creeps along the foreshore
and Dawe's point, a slender
stretch of steel away,
cannot be seen from self-perspective.
Above yachts and ferries
what tells of a point of view
that transcends the camera obscura of cells
as balanced, too, between opposing shores
dreams once built towards a central span
fall through webbing meant to withstand
the soot of further centuries.
   Of your death
thirty years of birth remain a shelter of sorts
and I can speak of solid structures
anchored struts, of tollways, railways
of scientists and imagists of space and style.
Even grass feels the weight of grief
not in the surface blades but in a deep shuddering
as though beneath the earth
the dead are forever forcing us to grow.
And I prefer to think of you as elected
to Tsvetaeva's stars
as the Honorable Member for Light.
A small group of bloodwoods decamp
and you're gone beneath the microscope

that makes memories larger, yachts smaller.
All day we built outwards from the shore
Bradfield said, *and the far shore*
vanished as we built.
This prickly harbour is the home of small birds.
The night's corona shines a brilliant green.
Mist nods like a soft religion.
And Lunar Park, closed.

Ceremony

One hand to her chest, the other
flat across a mint-green bible
the new citizen was photographed
swearing allegiance to the Queen of England.
That was in 1992 in Collingwood.
The mayoress gave everyone
a native plant, a plastic bag of roots.
The woman from Sarajevo was given a ti-tree
my friend from NZ a golden wattle
and over supper I overheard a Malaysian
woman say that she would like to plant
her tree in the bush somewhere
so that, if she moved house, her gift
would be safe - and then somebody asked
how she knew which part of the bush would be safe
from fire or development and did that mean
she would be needing advice concerning Australian
property law - and then another friend
presented her with the biggest bright bunch
of kangaroo paw and I noticed how everyone
seemed to like her and want to help.
But that was in 1992, in Collingwood.
That was before the ceremony was over
and the hall emptied. On the floor, left behind,
lay all the plastic flags
people had dropped in their hurry.

The Question Mark

Ear-lobe studded with a jewel
perhaps a diamond or a single milky pearl
to feminise the statement or express doubt
such as "In the beginning God created...?"

Quite a handy hook to hang
enquiry on, a single drop of blood
trailing from the amputated shoulder
of what is known now and forgotten next...

It is the "half-womb" of speech
the jester, the sarcastic priest
signifying "future" more efficiently than
a church pew of devout exclaiming cousins.

In the anonymous ancestry of marks
it is the eccentric aunt the family would prefer
to forget, she who having fallen into disrepute
swaggers, always, with attitude.

Casino

I

Rumours will not be believed.
I know I'll never win enough
or win when enough is needed.
Desire is the dream of elsewhere
and elsewhere the Eden of gamblers.
All vagrancies of the heart
have been granted amnesty
all loss endured for the sake of grieving.
Rumours will not be believed
but can we trust yet
the weird sciences of our future?
This roll, this deal, this incoherence -
when I reach into my pocket
it's all Star City, the Super Bucks
swilled and gleaming.
The jargon play takes a break
patrons numbing out by the loot fountain.
Their lips shine with Sic Bo sweat.
Free cokes swim flatly past
the tray crowd, inside, still
raging like a honeymoon at 2am.

II

The most pure lurching
human thing I do each morning
is to scheme, even in church
I daydream poker - red and black
are my blindnesses. The offertory
bell is a pay-out call, its grace note
the sound of coins clattering into
the holy plate- yet better.
Come to think of it
the priest's a gambling man
his livelihood a dicier game than mine.
Sorting the win, I roll the notes
tight as a big player
from the Monte Carlo Room.
While I'm head of St Vinnie's
I'd never pocket a cent of church money
but some nights it seems to me
that I've checked into a motel
that doesn't own a Bible
and even in dreams the blows
in the words of the croupiers
seem perfect.

III

All night, good friend
your Blackjack hands
have shuffled the cards
your Craps' six sided
one to six small dice
have landed, not caring much
what numbers mean.
If the dice are "hot"
you look at us
the shooters
with green felt eyes.
We have a wager for you
stickman
Hard Ten, Hard Four
your easy chatter
confirms our Odds On glory.
Here you come
holding hands with chance again.
We are gambling on transience
tearing through scars.
Bet the Line
anticipate the easy way
we are yours, we wait
for your two square bruises
to declare their scatter of stars.

IV

Why negotiate with me
I'm the unfaithful industry
sitting behind you
sharpening my claws.
In the grinning foyers
the sharks cruise and tackle
the place exists like an aquarium
in the dry ice clouds
the Dow Jones flattens
friable as a magic carpet
incredulous hope falls
through the fairytale...
even though the songs
chugalong for 24 hours a day
the invented world stalls
like smoke over Asia.

V

Let's not be overwrought.
Loneliness is a habit
a rusty tin can
a silly bones ghost.
I bail out my widowhood
and play the 5c machines.
I watch the bilge fill
with a new muddy thirst.

It's as easy as criticism
as welcome lights winking from porches.
In the morning I'll want to come again
to the bars and bells, the plums and the cherries.
I've got no spine.
I've got no centre.
The children say *pull up your socks*
tidy the till
you could after all if you wanted to.

Call it a hole in the bucket
a crack in the soul
an electrical fault
no Henry to fix it.
I won't mind too much
I'll forget the clinic.
I've got a wheel to spin
and detours to deal with.
Someone's throwing me
a meals-on-wheels ticket
but I don't want it.
I'm content with the drift
the microcosm of strangers
their voices like gravel
my gin & tonic minding
my machine, my people.

ALSO BY JENNIFER HARRISON *Black Pepper*

CABRAMATTA/CUDMIRRAH

A serious, ironic, uncompromising voice, occasionally reminding one of the poetry of Judith Wright.

- PETER ROSE, **Australian Book Review**

The richness and fascination of Harrison's brightly lit sea world are clearly evoked, along with the poet's feelings, transparent and reflecting.

- JENNIFER MILLER, **Social Alternatives**

MOSAICS & MIRRORS
COMPOSITE POEMS

(with Graham Henderson & K.F. Pearson)

The blended sensibilities of the Melbourne poets have in quite a number of instances produced an effect as pleasing and harmonious as any poet working in solitude could have managed... the Rose Hotel experiment has resulted in something of genuine interest and value.

- MICHAEL COSTIGAN, **Australian Book Review**

MICHELANGELO'S PRISONERS

This initial mid-life publication recalls Gwen Harwood's 1963 emergence, and Harrison seems to me to have other affinities with that formidable poetic talent.

- JENNIFER STRAUSS, **Australian Book Review**

Above all, these poems are fresh...They are not fashionable, they gesture nowhere; they are too deeply attentive to the strangeness they have found in the world..This is a fabulous, wise, superbly crafted book.

- ALAN GOULD, **Quadrant**

Black Pepper SPECIAL EDITIONS

THE HANGING OF JEAN LEE JORDIE ALBISTON
In this richly imagined procession of poems, Albiston re-imagines how the grim life of Jean Lee stepped along its course to her execution. The book is a triumph of grasp and sympathy.
- CHRIS WALLACE-CRABBE

THE GENIUS OF HUMAN IMPERFECTION JACK HIBBERD
Jack Hibberd has produced a distinctly original and enjoyable collection of poems - his poetic is to do with rhythm, sharp-edged language, proverbial utterance, oracle. His humour is wry and sensual, a form of the intellect in its wooing shape. The raunchy side of this collection gets broader as it progresses, especially in "Camperdown Dichotomies", a scabrous sequence which imagines from moral Melbourne a Sydney bequeathed by Cavafy. I recommend all into whose hands these poems pass to read *The Genius of Human Imperfection* with care.

These poems give pleasure, and there can never be too much skill at large in the world.
- PETER PORTER

MELBOURNE ELEGIES K.F. PEARSON
Melbourne Elegies being an adaptation and extension of Goethe's *Römische Elegien* is K.F. Pearson's sixth collection. The sensibility is fascinating, with the shadow of the German poet in Melbourne. It is a very sexy book; hardly anyone is willing to be tender about another person. There is nothing like it in Australian poetry

Black Pepper POETRY

ALBUM OF DOMESTIC EXILES ANDREW SANT
These poems are inviting, with an ease of rhythm. Their tone is conversational, yet notable for a quizzical and analytic teasing out of resonance. They question the nature of the place we call home.

THE SHADOW'S KEEP JOHN ANDERSON
A radical text; its language honed, subtle, yet volatile. The dreamlines, a single line form, came to the author in dreams and draw on Western psychology, Aboriginal and Japanese poetry traditions. Pantoums, fashioned from the dreamlines, achieve a formal grace and a powerful lyric intensity. The author's essay is a fascinating description of the genesis of this strange and tantalising work.

FILTH AND OTHER POEMS HUGH TOLHURST
A recurring motif is the cocktail of drugs, drink, sex and cynicism. The author's gift is to remain elegantly distanced, thus opening up our perceptions. His "Unfaithful Translations" from Catullus are outrageous satire; anarchic poems closely resembling party scenes. Witty, talented and accomplished.

THE BLUE GATE ALISON CROGGON
The writing shows a strong physicality, a constant feeling of lyrical sensuality and an overall dexterity and richness. Experiences, expressed through the delicate skin of the self, have resonance for others. Remarkable for its technical awareness of earlier poets.

THE WILD REPLY EMMA LEW
Dramatic in its scale and intensity, this collection of uncommon strength speaks with defiant gesture and powerful assertion. A

quirky, idiosyncratic approach to experience and language results in a poetry that makes for compulsive reading.

BOTANY BAY DOCUMENT JORDIE ALBISTON
Imbued with strong emotion these dramatic monologues are a rare and robust engagement with the events, conditions, language and cadences of an earlier period, based on wide ranging historical research. Eschewing sentimentality and keeping to the earthier view of women, the poems achieve the difficult miracle of being memorably present both in their time and ours.

CABRAMATTA/CUDMIRRAH JENNIFER HARRISON
"Cabramatta" remakes the author's youth, with its working class family values, in the patois of CB radio. "Cudmirrah" is a dialectic of memory and forgetting, where the brightly lit sea world of childhood holidays is evoked with richness and fascination. Restraint and detail are perfectly matched, the author drawing on her scientific background and studies of oceanography. A serious, ironic and uncompromising voice, impressing with its intelligence and containment.

THE APPARITION'S DAYBOOK K.F. PEARSON
This book length sequence, revealing a deep and sophisticated insight into the human condition, creates the equivocal and inviting figure of the Apparition. Unapologetically sexy, urbane and worldly wise he slips through the seams of the social world. The power of the verse evokes both tenderness and pathos, a book that lingers, like longing.

SENTENCES OF EARTH AND STONE
LOUIS DE PAOR
Written in Gaelic and accompanied by the author's English translations. Bewitching poetry of love, history and memory, its kernel quintessentially Irish. A shifting pattern of light and dark that is as visual as it is metaphorical. Love poems of such tenderness they take the breath away.

THE FOREST SET OUT LIKE THE NIGHT
JOHN ANDERSON

A work of extraordinary originality and quality which charts a new psychic frontier between the cultures of Aboriginal and White Australia. A brilliantly conceived meditation on place and being, a uniquely Australian song cycle.

MOSAICS & MIRRORS
JENNIFER HARRISON, GRAHAM HENDERSON AND K.F. PEARSON

This blend of distinctive talents defies the post-Romantic idea of the individual author, engages the emotions, confronts alienation and celebrates friendship and love. A unique experiment which has resulted in a work of interest and value.

AN AUSTRALIAN CONFERENCE OF THE BIRDS
ANNE FAIRBAIRN

Middle Eastern and Australian imagery and consciousness are flawlessly blended in this delightful tribute to the Sufi poem "The Conference of the Birds". Rich in insight and spiritual wisdom, exquisite in its use of language, the narrative blends imagery and metaphor as it takes flight.

PASSION & WAR K.F. PEARSON

This assured poet's verse biographies precede his powerful and sensitive translations of the extraordinary imagistic Spanish lyric poetry, forming a portrait of a nation consumed by civil war.

MICHELANGELO'S PRISONERS
JENNIFER HARRISON

A disciplined and intellectual lyricism illuminates her subjects. The poems give the sense of emerging out of an intractable element, language - experience, while being conscious of their emergence. A fabulous, wise, superbly crafted book.

Black Pepper FICTION

A PICTURE OUT OF FRAME MAMMAD AIDANI
A boy grows up in poverty in Khorramshahr, near the Persian Gulf, matures and goes to the capital, but the village life so lovingly portrayed holds a tragedy. The true pathos of the work lies in the healing that the central character attempts to create. The intuitive grasp of the way feeling holds the story together makes it live all the way through.

KICKING IN DANGER ALAN WEARNE
A comic masterpiece in the form of a detective novel. A rich brew of sporting Australia, a kind of 'Roman a Clef' of the importance of football in Melbourne culture.

LETTERS FROM BYRON JIM WILLIAMS
A beguiling comment on Byron Bay's weird and wonderful cultural mix, the author's letters reveal his natural talent as a storyteller in a series of enigmatic yet strangely satisfying tales.

AND THE WINNER IS... JON WEAVING
Eighteen winning stories from the Alan Marshal Awards combine with discussions by well known writers, using the stories to reveal the different aspects of the writer's craft.

THE SET-UP JOHN VASILAKAKOS
A psychological thriller and a study in individual and group paranoia based on the Greek Social Security scandal in Sydney in the late 70s.

NAVIGATIO ALISON CROGGON
The boundaries of fiction, non-fiction and poetry are blurred in

this feat of memory and imagination. Part autobiography, part family history, this thoughtful journey tells of late eighteenth century and also contemporary migration and settlement.

GIFTS & SORROWS RAPHAELLE POMIAN
Discrete and bittersweet stories which vividly bring to life the school and home life of girls growing up in France in the late 60's. A sensitive and honest depiction of some of the more painful experiences of childhood.

MEDIATIONS OF A FLAWED GROOM
VIVIAN HOPKIRK
Forceful and satirical action from a powerful but anarchic talent. The novel traverses the internal landscape of the narrator's mind whilst imprisoned for disorderly behavior.

DIARY OF A DWARF GRAHAM HENDERSON
These four novellas arrestingly reek of the insane and the unrequitedly erotic. Laughter and despair reveal the tragic scope of the clown.

SAILING THROUGH THE AMBER
SUSAN HANCOCK
Compellingly human stories of breathless emotional depth and uncanny observation which chart the disturbances of relationships and the ecstasy and pain of love.

THE PRISONER GAINS A BLURRED SKIN
NICHOLAS PLAYFORD
Vividly drawn stories of citizens of Australian society hauntingly shift the reader's view of the commonplace. The stylistic flamboyance and pleasure in the texture of language is reminiscent of Beckett's early fiction.

Titles are available from good bookstores or may be ordered directly from *Black Pepper*